The Quick and Dirty Guide

to Overcoming Infidelity

By Deirdre Haynes, Ed.S, LPCS, NCC, DCC

Dear Reader,

Thank you so much for purchasing **The Quick and Dirty Guide to Overcoming Infidelity!** Infidelity is one of the hardest things to get over in any relationship. Your trust has been betrayed, what you cherished has been destroyed, and your relationship is holding on by a thread. All may seem to be lost.

However, there is always hope! If you and your partner are willing to put in the work, your broken relationship can be discarded, and a new, stronger relationship can be created!

This book is in no way a definitive, all-inclusive guide on the causes and eventual effects of infidelity. However, it was written to give a quick and dirty, straight to the point account of what some of the causes of infidelity are and how broken relationships can be healed.

As a Licensed Professional Counselor, I have worked with many couples that were dealing with infidelity. Many were able to work through the tough times, together, and eventually heal themselves and the relationship.

Please note that If your individual efforts do not improve the relationship then I recommend entering couples/marriage counseling. Many men and women have personally told me that having a "mediator" of sorts who can see both sides of the story really helped them to understand their partner's thought processes as well as their own.

With all of that said, let's begin….

Sincerely,

Deirdre F. Haynes, Ed.S, LPCS, NCC, DCC

Chapters

Chapter One: The Love Story

Chapter Two: Problems Areas

Chapter Three: Infidelity: Setting The stage

Chapter Four: Infidelity: The Act

Chapter Five: Infidelity: Exposure!

Chapter Six: Infidelity: After the Exposure

Chapter Seven: Overcoming Infidelity: Where do we go from here?

Chapter One

The Love Story

We all love a great love story. So often, we learn how relationships work from watching love stories on television. You know how it goes. A person meets someone when they least expect it. Both of them are on their best behaviors and are displaying all the good qualities they have to offer. The chemistry is electric and they sincerely miss each other when the other person is not around. Time goes on and love steps into the room. Everything is wonderful as they bear and raise children together and ride off into the sunset.

Le sigh….how beautiful! This is where I would insert the emoji with heart-shaped eyes if I could. Falling in love with someone is a truly beautiful thing but it rarely turns out the way it is depicted in the movies. That is not to say that you can't have a loving long-term relationship and eventually ride off into the sunset. You can. However, long-term relationships usually require a lot of sacrifice and a lot of breaking down and rebuilding.

Most people get caught up in or even addicted to the **Honeymoon Phase** of the relationship. The Honeymoon phase of the relationship starts at the beginning of the relationship and lasts for about six months to a year. This is the period when the object of your affection can do no wrong. They are perfect in your eyes and vice versa. There is excitement about learning every little nuance about your partner. You want to know what makes them tick and what turns them off. You want to know their political and religious views. You are in the School of Love and you are absorbing everything you can about the one you are falling in love with on a daily basis.

The next phase after the Honeymoon phase is what I call the **Work Phase**. The Work phase starts after you have had your first argument/disagreement and you are now beginning to see things that you don't like and didn't notice before. Things like snoring, lack of a work ethic, no drive/ambition, different religious viewpoints, etc. are beginning to get on your nerves. You still love the person but you are trying to decide if this is truly the person for you.

I'm sure you have heard of the 80/20 rule. The 80/20 rule suggests that if the person you love possesses 80 percent of the traits that you need and want then it may be wise to accept the 20 percent of traits that you don't like or don't want. This works as long as the 20 percent does not consist of non-negotiables. A non-negotiable is something that goes against your core values or principles. For example, if a core belief or value for you is that all women should cook home cooked meals daily then that is a non-negotiable. You may try to overlook it for awhile but it will eventually take its toll on you because it is a core value of yours. So, non-negotiables should not be ignored.

When couples can work out the kinks in the Work phase then they will eventually enter the **Stabilization Phase**. During this phase, the partners begin to gel and flow together. A deeper more sustaining love evolves. This type of love is not based on how well you function in bed together or other superficial aspects, but it is based on mutual respect and understanding. I like to say that during this stage the partners will attest that they have been through some things but coming out of it together has brought them even closer.

What many people don't often realize is that relationships change over time. Like anything else people grow within a relationship. Sometimes they grow together and sometimes, unfortunately, they grow apart. What keeps a relationship sustainable is when both partners make room for their partner's growth and changes while remembering that they too are growing and changing. The sooner both parties in the relationship realize that there is an ebb and flow with every relationship and that each day is not going to be roses and butterflies, then it is much more likely that they will develop a loving and long-lasting relationship.

Chapter Two

Problem Areas

When people enter a relationship, they enter it with the goal of uniting and becoming one. That is the ultimate goal of any relationship, however, one must not forget about their individual identity. Many people enter relationships or even find themselves addicted to being in a relationship because they want to forget their individual identity. They have been so traumatized in their own life that they want to forget their individual self and merge with someone else.

As much as I understand the logic behind the idea of merging with the person you love, if it is an unhealthy alliance, then that merging is what I call a **Parasitic Relationship**. A Parasitic relationship is the same type of relationship that a parasite has with its host. The parasite latches onto the host (the partner) and sucks the life right out of the host. Think of a tick that latches on to a family pet. The pet (host) may not notice it for a very long time but the long-term effects will begin to harm the host's health and can even cause death!

A Parasitic relationship is no different. If one partner is running for dear life from his or her own identity and life then they will eventually wear the host partner down with their neediness, possessiveness, and drama.

So, I know you're asking, "Why would someone want to run away from their own life?" I'm glad you asked. There are a multitude of answers to that question. I will discuss a few below:

Childhood trauma- Childhood traumas run the gamut but can play a profound role in how a person behaves as an adult. Some examples of childhood trauma are below:

1. **<u>Daddy Issues-</u>** If daddy was missing in action or dysfunctional in some way then this will play a profound role in how your partner behaves. Men and women tend to suffer with abandonment issues if daddy was missing. Abandonment issues show up when they can't stand to be away from you for long periods of time to the point that you can't breathe. It also shows up when they feel that when you are mad with them you will leave them for good. They don't understand that just because you are angry with them doesn't mean that you are trashing the relationship and abandoning them.

2. **<u>Momma Issues</u>**- Momma issues affect men and women and tend to show up as laziness, perfectionism and/or workaholism. When a person feels that their momma never approved of them or they felt that they were never good enough for their momma, then they tend to become underachievers or overachievers. If momma abandoned the family then the same abandonment issues mentioned above may be present.

3. **<u>Abuse Issues</u>**- When a child is abused by either parent or family members, they tend to develop a skewed way of viewing the world. They never really feel safe in the world. They fear someone becoming mad at them because they never know when the next put-down, slap or kick is coming. When someone is angry with them, even though they fear losing them, they may immediately start a verbal or physical fight with their partner to "get it over with" or they may shut down completely and morph into their five or six-year-old self. Some people shut down completely when they sense the slightest irritation in their partner which is often irritating to their partner who may want to have a grown-up discourse with the person he or she is involved with or even married too. Many times, the person is dissociating. Dissociation means that their body is in the room, but their mind has shut down. This does not mean they have multiple personalities, but some people who have been abused learned quickly that "leaving their body" when abuse was taking place preserved their sanity.

4. **<u>Rapes/Molestations</u>**- People that have been abused sexually either by being molested, raped, or both also don't feel safe in the world. Their trust in people has been crushed usually at a young child. Many feel that not only has their virginity and purity been taken or destroyed but their ability to use their voice has been taken away. When your pleas for the offender to stop hurting you go unheeded, it is logical to begin to think that your voice doesn't matter. This results in people who either completely shut down sexually in relationships or they may be overly sexual and believe that sex is the only way to get someone to stop being angry with them.

Other Relationship Trauma- A person's experiences in prior relationships can and usually will rear its ugly head in their current relationship. Listed below are some examples of traumas that may have happened in a person's previous relationships:

1. **Liars and Cheaters**- Liars and cheaters often don't have a clue as to how much they can devastate a person that truly loved them. Interacting with someone that constantly lies to you while looking you in your eyes or who cheats on you every opportunity they get, can truly destroy a person's self-worth. Countless clients have sat before me wondering what is it about them that is not good enough to keep this person from lying to them and cheating on them. Their self-esteem has crumbled, and they feel and call themselves broken. Even though I reassure them that their partner's lying, and cheating is truly about their partner's selfishness and doesn't have anything to do with them, it is usually to no avail. Once they enter a new relationship, they become hypersensitive to everything their partner says which can become draining if their partner is not cheating. These are the people that check phones, texts, emails, and anything else they can get their hands on to prove to themselves whether or not their partner is cheating. That is an exhausting job! All the snooping will either yield what they are looking for or prove that their partner is innocent...this time.

2. **Domestic Violence-** When a person has been abused physically, verbally, and emotionally abused in a prior relationship, it will certainly be detrimental to a new relationship. Oftentimes, the abused will try to push their new partner to violence since this is the pattern of behavior they have learned to accept. The domestic violence pattern usually includes arguments that escalate into physical violence. After the physical violence has taken place, they then enter a honeymoon period in which the violent partner reassures

his/her partner that it will never happen again and attempts to prove how much they love them. Many people that have been abused seek violence because to them that out-of-control show of violence indicates how much their partner loves them. This is a sad but true phenomenon. This cycle of abuse will continue throughout the life of the victim until he or she makes a conscious decision to love himself or herself more than they love their partner. Only then, will the cycle end.

Chapter Three

Infidelity: Setting the Stage

In this chapter, I will discuss how the stage can be set and primed for an inevitable affair. Let me be clear, just because the following aspects may occur in any relationship, does not GUARANTEE that one or both partners will cheat. There are many couples that are very committed to their relationship and even if the following aspects are present, they refuse to cheat, and instead work harder on their relationship.

With that said, when one partner begins to allow the thoughts in their own head to override their logic, then problems begin to escalate in the relationship. In other words, when one person, allows their own past experiences to cloud their better judgment then these thoughts and insecurities can overwhelm them to the point that they may start harassing and accusing their partner of things they may not be guilty of doing. No one likes to be called a liar or to be told that they are doing something that they are not doing. Many partners will begin to "prove their innocence" by granting their partner access to their phone, text messages, and account information. This pattern of having to prove to their partner their innocence will eventually get old and often destroys the relationship all because of fantasies inside of their partner's head.

The stress of having to constantly prove, day in and day out, their innocence often becomes too much. During this time, they may decide to confide in their friends at work or their childhood friends to discuss all the turmoil their life is in and how unhappy they are with their current situation. At this point, they are still willing to work on the relationship but when all their efforts to prove their innocence fails, they will certainly begin to distance themselves from the accusations, stress and anger that is associated with the relationship.

The "work spouse" doesn't help the situation. Usually, the work spouse is someone that looks out for them on the job. They may be a listening ear or someone that brings them their favorite meal or cake to work. Many of these situations remain at work and nothing ever evolves from it. However, if the work spouse is a predator or someone that sees a vulnerable prey then he or she may take full advantage of that person's weakness and capitalize on the situation.

These people will be the listening ear, the friend and confident and they will say and do everything that the person's partner is not saying or doing in order to win that person over. This is a recipe for disaster but more on that later.

Being in any high-stress situation for a long period of time will take a toll on anybody. People tend to deploy defense mechanisms or ways to cope with the stress without even thinking about it.

Some examples of defense mechanisms that people use in high stress environments or situations, which should be red flags that the relationship is in jeopardy, are as follows:

1. Some people will begin to work more in an effort to stay away from home. Usually when they have a partner that continually complains about how unhappy they are, they will try to avoid that person in order to avoid feeling judged or that they can't do anything right. In other words, when home life is out of control, some people will seek the comfort, familiarity, and calmness of the work environment. Think about it. Who will really have something to say about someone working more and bringing home more money? So, they hide behind work in an effort to get away, have some sense of control of their life and to hear their own thoughts.

2. Some people will shut down emotionally. In the counseling arena, we call that emotional numbing. They become so desensitized to the drama and antics of their partner that they come off as simply cold and uncaring. It is not to say that they don't care but emotionally they are at their wit's end, so they go numb. They don't feel anything because they have built a wall around their heart to keep the hurt out.

3. Some people become even more needy and emotional when they feel distance from their partner. Remember when I talked about abandonment issues? When they do something that they know is pushing their partner away they become anxious and fearful that they are going to lose them, so they panic. Their panic manifests in becoming needier and possibly attention-seeking. Their antics tends to turn their partner off even more which

generates an even greater emotional response. This cycle continues until the person's worst fears manifest and their partner decides to leave or do something that prompts them to have to leave.

Many people see these red flags waving a mile away and yet they still can't control their impulses in order to avoid impending doom.

Chapter Four

Infidelity: The Act

So, the relationship is on its last leg and both partners are feeling the strain. Something must give. If an intervention of some sort (i.e. therapy, heart-to-heart discussions, a break from the relationship, etc.) doesn't occur then something is bound to happen. For many, infidelity happens. Someone makes the conscious and sometimes not so conscious decision to get his or her needs met outside of the relationship.

Some people develop online friendships via websites that result in sexual trysts. To many, this method provides them with the attention and sexual release that they are missing without the emotional attachment. They still love their partner, but they feel that they need to be able to release stress by temporarily embracing a fantasy world with someone that will not interfere in their relationship.

The work spouse may become the object of desire when the partner feels that their relationship is out of control and is not ready to deal with the emotional toll that the relationship has taken on them. They may become closer to the work spouse by divulging more and more information about how unhappy they are in their relationship. The work spouse, predator, can use this information to become everything that the partner at home is not. He or she may say and do all the right things to make the object of their desire see that they deserve better and that they can be just the person to give it to them.

The work spouse may initiate trysts while at work or plan to hook up when they go on a work-related trip together. Either way, the excitement of experiencing something new along with feeling understood by the work spouse can cause a person to jump headfirst into a forbidden situationship with the work spouse. This relationship may seem perfect at first but all good things must come to an end. More on that later.

Sometimes a partner will reach out to a past love or lover for their emotional needs. They may reach out to someone that really loved them or felt that they were the best thing going in order to remember who they were prior to getting into their current relationship. This can result in another type of predator taking advantage of a vulnerable person (prey).

Please note that when I describe work spouses and former loves/lovers as predators, I am not condoning or approving of the behavior of the partner. At the end of the day, they are in a relationship and whether they consciously or unconsciously make a decision to cheat, a decision was most certainly made.

Chapter Five

Infidelity: Exposure!

Everything in the dark will come to the light. That saying has held true through the centuries. Therefore, there is no need to search for "evidence" to prove that someone is cheating. It can literally hit you over the head like a client described when a box containing love letters did when he was least expecting it!

Most people find out about affairs in a happenstance way. Those that seek information may find what they are looking for but because of their means of attaining the information they will talk them out of believing the very information they fought so hard to find. This is why I tell my clients that if you are going to drive yourself crazy searching and looking for "evidence" to prove their partner's guilt then be prepared to do something about it if you find something. Many are not ready to take action so there is no need of hunting down information and driving your possibly innocent partner crazy.

So, how does one find out about a cheating partner? As I said before it is usually by happenstance. They may be minding their own business and running errands when suddenly they see their partner with someone else walking down the street or eating in a restaurant. They could innocently answer their partner's phone while they are in the shower only to find themselves talking to the "other woman or other man" on the line.

Many have said that almost by Divine Providence, their partner's Facebook or social media account remained open long after it should have shut down and closed, only to find sexually explicit inbox messages with the person they are cheating with at work or in the community. This has also happened with email accounts that remained open long enough for the partner to wander by and take a look at the inbox messages their partner has been sending and receiving.

They may find a receipt for roses, jewelry, a hotel they never visited or even food receipts at restaurants they haven't visited. Their bank statements may indicate these purchases or show large, cash withdrawals out of their bank account.

A couple people have found hidden items within the family home that indicate correspondence with a lover that may live out of town. While sometimes it is the family friend that bravely tells him or her that their partner has been seen around town or coming out of a hotel with a person that did not look like him or her.

Some of the most devastating ways that a person may find out about infidelity is by contracting an STD. This may be something minor that they can get rid of or it may a life-threatening, long-term STD that is not only devastating emotionally but physically.

Still yet, some may find out because their partner is forced to tell them since they have gotten the outside lover (mistress or Miss Stress) pregnant and a baby is on the way. This is the ultimate betrayal because not only has the person cheated but they have brought an outside life in their world that will be a part of both of their lives forever.

Any of these exposures can be absolutely devastating to a partner. The truth is staring them in the face and they have some serious decisions to make.

Chapter Six

Infidelity: After the Exposure

Time heals all wounds. That adage has also been around for centuries and still applies even today. As much as the hurting partner does not want to hear those comforting words, they are still the truth. Time can heal any wound...as long as you let it.

After the infidelity has been exposed, both partners may go through a wide range of emotions. For the most part, the partner that has been exposed will probably go through the Grieving Process. When I counsel my clients, I tend to discuss Kubler-Ross' Grief Cycle. Please note that everyone is different, so they may not follow the cycle exactly but for the most part they will spend some time in each phase of the cycle.

The first phase is the **Denial Phase**. This is a time when the person immediately goes into a period of disbelief. They have to almost pinch themselves to make sure that what happened really happened. In this stage, there is often avoidance of their partner and others, confusion about exactly what happened, shock that their partner was capable of doing this to them and possibly fear that their relationship is going to end after, so much time and effort has been put into it.

The next phase is usually the **Sadness/Depression Phase**. Kubler-Ross tends to state that anger happens next, but it has mostly been my experience that sadness occurs. In this state the person may feel overwhelmed by their mixed emotions. They may feel helpless to change the fate of the relationship. They can also feel hostility toward their partner and/or take flight in an effort to avoid seeing their partner.

The next phase is the **Anger Phase**. The person has grown weary of crying and has become angry at himself or herself for not seeing the signs or they may be angry with their partner for betraying their trust when they thought everything was fine. During this phase they may experience frustration, irritation, and anxiety.

The next phase is the **Bargaining Phase**. During this phase, the betrayed person may struggle to find meaning for the betrayal. They may wonder what they could have done to keep that person from cheating. He or she may reach out to family or friends to vent their frustrations as well as to get advice on what they did wrong in the relationship. The guilty partner will often become angry at their partner for spreading their personal business and/or for "dragging their name through the mud". This is a normal reaction but oftentimes the partner seeking advice isn't intentionally trying to hurt them, but they are looking for validation.

The last phase is the **Acceptance Phase**. The partner will eventually, over time, come to a place where they are ready to explore their options, put a new plan in place for the relationship or decide that it is time for them to move on emotionally or physically.

The guilty partner, the one that cheated, will have his or her own set of emotions. He or she may also go through the grieving cycle as the couple works out what lead to his or her infidelity. He or she may also get stuck in the anger phase because they may feel attacked and belittled to the point that they can't take anymore. A valid question that is often asked is, "How long must I pay for what I did?" That is a powerful question and it is one that must be answered in order for the relationship to move forward.

Chapter Seven

Overcoming Infidelity:

Where do we go from here?

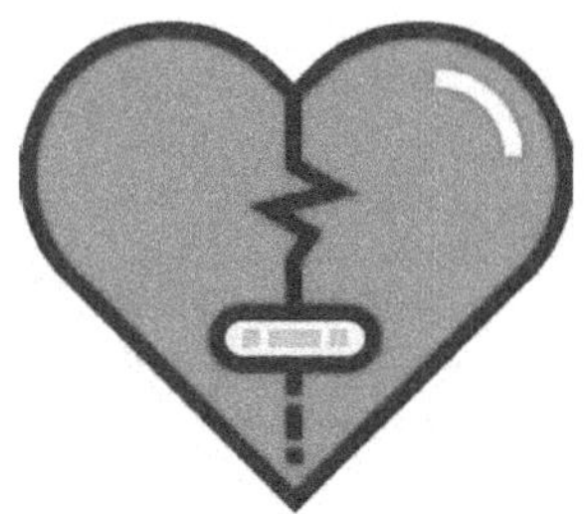

Overcoming infidelity is one of the hardest things for a person to deal with and overcome in a relationship. It is simply hard. Everything they believe in or thought about the relationship comes into question.

As I stated before, the betrayed partner will enter the grieving cycle and the way that they handle that stress will depict whether or not the relationship will survive the betrayal.

Oftentimes, the betrayed partner will start to berate his or her partner in an effort to shed the unwanted emotions that flood their brain and body. On some levels this is understandable, and the guilty partner must be willing to stand in all of his or her shame and deal with it. However, verbal and emotional abuse is unacceptable. There are limits and time limits to how much the betrayed partner gets to dump his or her negative emotions onto the guilty partner. That limit should be decided by your internal signals. You will know when enough is enough.

Look at it this way, if the guilty partner was a child and he or she did something that you totally don't agree with such as using drugs, stealing, having a baby out of wedlock, or getting in trouble at school, how long would you punish them? Forever is out of the question. So, do you punish them and/or give them verbal tongue lashings for years on end because of their poor choices?

Recognizing that you are hurt, mad, and you feel betrayed, I still must ask how much is enough? The partner that cheated has decisions to make as well. How much will they take because there needs to be boundaries? Yes, there is a level of reparations (making up for what you did) that needs to occur and there is a level of asking your partner what they need you to do to make them feel better and begin to heal from what I did. However, there still needs to be boundaries and time limits. In the beginning, this may mean that you need to show your call log, keep your phone unlocked, answer questions (sometimes over and over) honestly and openly or even call to let them know where you are at different times of the day, in order to rebuild trust.

With that said, the key is that this should occur FOR A PERIOD OF TIME only! It cannot, and it will not go on indefinitely.

So, when someone cheats:

1. You must, eventually, make the decision to forgive. When you forgive someone, you are making a conscious decision to let it go. If thoughts about your partner cheating again or fears about your partner hurting you again, come to mind then you have to learn to soothe yourself. Yes, when we are angry it may feel great to yell, fuss, curse, and get it all out but you are destroying the person you say that you love. So how can you love something and destroy it at the same time and expect them to believe it? They won't. After you allow yourself to grieve as long as you need to grieve then you have to make the decision to forgive and begin the process of either healing the relationship or begin the process of letting the relationship go. The only requirement at this point is that you cannot allow yourself to remain stuck and to wallow in the hurt and pain of the broken relationship. All things have to come to an end.

2. To begin the healing process, you have to make a tough decision. You have to decide whether you are going to stay or leave. This decision should be entirely up to you. Others can offer advice, but you have to do what your heart tells you to do.

3. If you make the conscious decision to stay, then you forfeit the right to punish your partner forever by accusing him or her of cheating every time they are out of your eyesight. Becoming overly possessive, jealous, suspicious, etc. is a recipe for disaster. If you are going to do this, then it is better to let that person go because continuous accusations are a form of emotional and verbal abuse. When you decide to stay, you make the decision to take ownership of your own pain.

4. On the other hand, some people make the extremely difficult decision to let their partner go because they simply can't get past or over the betrayal. That is one of the most difficult decisions a person can make especially when they still love their partner, but it is a healthy and honorable decision. If your heart and soul feels as if you cannot get over it, then you simply can't get over it. Your partner may be hurt or even devastated but they

eventually they will respect your decision. That is a loving decision because the alternative could result in you destroying your partner because you may try to inflict the level of pain you feel on them day after day and year after year. That is emotional abuse and it's not right. Love them enough to let them go.

5. Both parties must understand that if the two of you decide to stay in the relationship and work it out then you are now working on a new relationship/marriage. The old relationship/marriage died when the trust was broken.

6. There is a saying that, "You can have anything you want but you have to be willing to pay the price." If you want the relationship to work, then a price must be paid. The guilty party must allow the betrayed party to ask questions, express his or her hurt, and deal with moments of rejection in order to atone for the past transgression. This is a natural part of healing. To suggest that your partner must simply get over it and move on is not only cold but heartless. If you are guilty, you must give your partner space to heal.

7. Both parties will have to make sacrifices. One partner may have to give their time, their ear, their compassion, their body, etc. to their partner at times when they don't feel like it. Your partner may need you to be emotionally and physically present for them even when you don't want to be in the same room with them. Every situation is different and there are times that you simply may not be able to push through to be there for your partner, but if you decided to stay, they you will have to push through those blocks in order to move your relationship forward.

8. The sacrifices cannot be one-sided. Both partners have to make sacrifices for each other out of love. As I said before, there may be times when you just don't have it in you to give at that moment but if your partner needs you then instead of taking another opportunity to bring up their infidelity, maybe you need to stop, get out of your own feelings, and ask what do they need from you in that moment and vice versa.

9. Heal thyself. You have to put in the work to heal that broken part of you. Healing after infidelity is a walk that you have to walk alone. No amount of abusing your partner- emotionally, physically, sexually, etc. will stop your pain. You have to do the work and take ownership of your pain. Your partner is not able to heal you or push your broken pieces back together. You have to do that! That is your job. They can help by being there for you and being supportive but that is all they can really do. Healing after infidelity is 75 percent internal work and 25 percent work with your partner. An example of this is how you feel when someone you know and loved passes away. Your partner may feel bad about the situation. They may truly feel as if their heart may break for you because you are hurt or devastated by the death of someone you truly loved. You had memories with this person and experiences with this person but to expect someone to feel exactly like you feel will never happen. You have to accept the fact that they don't know how you feel. That is a walk you have to walk by yourself. No one can walk the walk for you. The same concept applies to your healing after someone has cheated on you. They will definitely feel guilty about what they did and even shameful, but they cannot feel the pain that you feel. So, it is up to you to heal your own wound. Sadly, we often expect too much from other people. We expect them to feel what we feel and to help us heal when that is our job.

10. You must decide what your new relationship/marriage will look like in the future. If communication was lacking, then this is the time to really work on understanding what your partner is saying and their thought processes behind what they are saying. Also, take the time to discover their love language. That thing that your partner continues to badger you about such as spending more time with them, cleaning the house, touching or kissing them or telling them that you think they are the bomb.com are all ways that they fill their love tank. Listen to them and check out the love languages assessment at www.5lovelanguages.com.

11. When someone cheats, if you decide to stay with them then you have to get to a point where you work through the problems of not having intimacy. You're hurt, and you may get to a point that you can't touch your partner without thinking of what they did with someone else. That is perfectly normal. However, once you say you are going to stay in the relationship then you can't hold your partner hostage in a sexless relationship. You have to push yourself to re-establish intimacy in the relationship. If you don't and your partner acclimates to sleeping on the couch or in the spare bedroom, then the relationship is doomed to fail.

12. With that said, true intimacy has nothing to do with sex. True intimacy is to withhold the sex and rebuild the intimacy that has been lost. True intimacy is holding hands, looking into each other's eyes, cuddling in bed without having sex, and being able to connect on an emotional level. Many couples start off believing that if they are mad with each other, and they have sex, then they will both feel good and the problem will be solved. If your relationship is built only on your bedroom chemistry, then expect many problems down the line. Please note, that it is not just men behaving in this manner. Some women have been programmed to think that way as well. Usually that is due to them being taught that sex will make it better and sex will calm their partner down and make them forget all about what happened.

13. You have to realize that you are on the same team. Just realize it. Taking the time to talk about the hard stuff as it occurs. Learning to laugh together and to see each other for the wounded yet strong people you are will go a long way in repairing the relationship.

14. Seek professional couples or marriage counseling if your individual efforts are not working and before you give up on your relationship.

Listed below are some of the other books written by Deirdre Haynes:

The Vault	**The Vault: Therapist's Edition**
The Vault: Anxiety Edition	**The Vault: Depression Edition**
The Vault: Journal for Women	**The Vault: Journal for Men**
The Vault: Gratitude Journal	**The Big Book of Communications**
The Vault: Group Therapy Edition	

Blindspots: Everything you DIDN'T know you needed to know about starting a Mental Health Practice